I Can And I Will

RICK STANFIELD

DEDICATION

I dedicate "I Can And I Will" to my church family at A Simple Faith. Tina, Ricky, and I walked into this church one day and our lives forever changed because we did. These people are my family now and their kindness and love will never be forgotten.

I CAN AND I WILL

RICK STANFIELD

ACKNOWLEDGEMENT

I want to express my sincere gratitude to the following people who, without their support, knowledge, work, and input, this book would never been completed.

First and most important, my wife Tina, who held this family together when most people would walked away from the situation, and focused on themselves. She didn't. She took a deep breath, dug in, and battled for her family and I'll never forget it.

When you don't have a clue how to assemble a marketable book, it takes a small army of people with supernatural talent to help and that's exactly what God blessed me with. I can't explain how talented Tim Ryals and Ronnie McBrayer are, so I won't even try. All I can say is thank you and the kindness and work you put into this, with nothing in exchange will never be forgotten.

The talent of Amanda Rhodes, who created the illustrations for this book, completely blew me away.

Thank you, Bridget Bergwall, Deborah Wheeler, Karen Snyder, and Deb Tyson who tirelessly read my writings and corrected my grammar, as well as my other stupid mistakes.

I am grateful to my mother and father for not being normal. Your uniqueness, unconditional love, and creativity helped me become the person I am today.

Although I took a twisted route to my current place in life, without the combination of your DNA, I would be lost in a sea of normal.

During these horrible times, my son Ricky stepped up to the plate and showed what type of human being he is. He was a teenager with everything one day and his life completely changed, seemingly overnight. He lost his vehicle, his home, and actually cleaned houses with us, to help his family survive. He never complained one time. Thank you and I am so proud of the man he has become.

Thank you Emmilou and Ricky Stanfield III. The love they show me, just by holding my hand, a quick look, and hearing them say Papa, has enabled me to love others more than I ever would have been able to without them.

I am eternally grateful to and love you all.

Rick Stanfield

CONTENTS

INTRODUCTION

I had never felt fear like this before in my life, and as I looked at Tina, I could see the terror in her eyes too. I remember thinking "How did we get here? How the hell did this happen to us?".

It was 2 o'clock in the morning and the darkness was powerfully frightening. I could see Tina's face every time the lightening flashed and she looked terrified. The rain was pouring from the sky and the sound of that rain was deafening. Our car had a quarter of a tank of gasoline and we had $19.70 to our names.

Then, all of a sudden, the rain began to come inside the car like a waterfall coming through the roof. Tina and I scooted toward the center of the car holding on to each other tight, and you could almost feel the wheels of our minds working on how to get out of this mess.

It wasn't the sound of thunder or the flashing of the lightening that scared me. It was the uncertainty and knowing that we didn't have a home to go to. It was the desperate feeling of inadequacy because we had to send our son to his friend's house as we tried to figure out what to do.

As terrified as we were that night, I still remember the smell of an overheated car and motor oil, but mostly, the aroma of a fresh rain that was overwhelmingly calming. It's funny how God can send something to you in a time of need -- something so simple as the smell of a summer rain.

- Rick Stanfield

But before I get started telling my story of how we went from homelessness to owning a successful company, I want to thank God for my wife, Tina, and my son, Ricky. These two amazing people have supported me and shown a loyalty and a boundless love that I do not deserve. Families are often tested and many times, they fall apart when things get tough. A strong heavenly bond has been created between us that can never be broken. I am so blessed to actually know the level of love they have for me, in good times and bad. Many people say they will do anything for you, but these two have proven it. Now, I promise to spend the rest of my life proving my love for them.

My family's 10 Days of sleeping in a car taught me so many life lessons that I'm eager to share with everyone what I learned, in hopes that what I learned can in turn help someone else. This guide to solving problems that I am going to present can be applied to almost any situation you're facing and if I could have figured out these solutions years ago, it would have made my life a lot easier.

We all have periods in our lives when it seems like the cards are stacked against us, or we've made the universe angry. It's probably because the cards were stacked against you and you did anger the universe. In my case, I wanted to blame the cards or the universe, but I was the one who chose the cards and I was the one that broke the universe's rules, and that is what I came to understand. As soon as I chose the correct cards to deal and be dealt and listened to the Creator of the Universe, I figured out how to find happiness.

During this time frame of my life, I had to figure out how to get my family and me to the next day alive. Although I did have others to turn to, it seemed like I didn't, so in desperation, I turned to God for the first time in my life. If I hadn't figured this out quickly, I would never have made it through, and certainly would have never found the satisfaction, peace, and success that I have now.

My story is a little different than many, as it is more extreme than most people encounter, but you can take the same principles and answers that God provided me and apply them to the situation you're facing.

Those 10 Days of my life have given me the ability to live a happy, genuinely fulfilled life that I never would have had without them and I'm eager to teach this simple life guide to others. If you are experiencing the same type of monetary crisis that I did, let me show you how to prioritize certain areas of your life, the money you need will come. Once you stop worshiping money and making it the reason for your actions, it becomes a fruit of your dedication to God. It's your mindset that is key to success. I don't believe I am unique. I believe what I learned will help anyone.

If you're a CEO of a Fortune 500 Company, or you're homeless, I believe this guide will lead you to a life that you're proud of, and more importantly, that God is proud of. These simple principles can be used to work your way out of any situation you're in.

During those 10 days, I started praying many times a day – something I had never done before – and the answer to every one of those day's issues, and there were many, were given to me.

Some simple ethics such as hard work, determination, and hope are so cliché, but if applied correctly, they work.

Each of those days, I had to examine the circumstance, take what answers God provided for me, and apply that answer to the situation. Before long I figured out that He had given me those answers a long time ago, but I wasn't listening. Now, I was listening and it was working.

Thinking back through my life, I came to realize that the answers to the problems I faced were so simple, but I made them difficult by trying to justify my way of life. If I had read a book like this prior to my troubles, I believe the troubles would not have happened.

Let me help you find the life that we are all looking for – the life that God intended for us to live. We all have a calling in life that He has instilled into our Heavenly makeup that we must find. I believe this is mine.

CHAPTER ONE
THE BEGINNING

This book is about the hard-learned keys I learned to living a happy, stable, and successful life. But, I firmly believe that God always knew that I would go through the tough time that I went through, and that I would need the right life partner to successfully make it out to the other side where He wanted me. This is a key component for everyone.

God gave me my first glimpse of my future life partner when I was in the fifth grade when I saw a little blonde-haired girl sitting in the back of my fifth-grade class.

I had no idea who she was. She looked shy, but, what I remember most is her being the most beautiful person I had ever seen in my long 9 years on earth.

This was 1979 and somehow I knew that I would marry this girl in a few years. Little did we all know that we were about to go for one hell of a ride over the next 30 years, but, I now know that God did.

Tina and I married when we were 18 years old, and we had our only son, Ricky Jr., when we were 19, and both got jobs in our little hometown of Steele, Missouri. In my family, you automatically became a police officer when you turned 21 years old. My grandfather and father were both police officers, so it seemed natural to follow in their footsteps.

One of the best law enforcement agencies in the world is the Missouri State Highway Patrol, so, I knew that if I was going to be a police officer, this is who I wanted to work for. I applied for and was accepted into the Missouri State Highway Patrol where I spent the next few years working as a state trooper and an agent with the Division of Drug and Crime Control. However, we both wanted more for our family.

One night, while working a late shift, I met my Sergeant, Bob Ross, for a midnight snack. We talked about money -- and he knew a lot about money. He was my hero. He worked as a state trooper, but was extremely successful flipping houses. In fact, he should be recognized for inventing that title because he was "flipping houses" before anyone had ever even coined the title yet.

My dad had always taught me to listen to someone who had accomplished the task that they were teaching you about. Dad explained that if someone who has no money is explaining how to make money, most likely, their advice is not reliable. In this case, I was young, and probably more than anything, I wanted to make money.

That night, while eating catfish and French fries that had to have been cooked the day before, Bob told me that everyone wants to make money, but only a few do it. The difference is that those few who make it act on what they talk about. Everyone talks about money, and many even share their ideas on how to do it, but few people take that leap from the security of a 9 to 5 job. We discussed all kinds of ways to prosper, but none sounded better than selling a house.

After we left that diner, we drove to Bob's house where he gave me a "for sale" sign and I put it in my front yard. I had paid $44,000 for the house that Tina, Ricky and I lived in and I ended up selling it for $55,000 a few months later. Wow! I had the bug after that. I wanted to do it again and I did. And again. And again.

Before long, Tina and I were building new houses and selling them as soon as they were built. We were young, very young, and didn't save much money, but were extremely prosperous as the money kept coming in.

The advice that Bob Ross had given me was exactly right. Even though, later in my life, after everything had happened to us, money was not a priority in my life any longer, I used the advice that Bob had given me regarding "acting". I knew that it wasn't enough to want anything, whatever that "want" was. I learned that I had to act to achieve.

At this point, I decided it might work with my schedule better to ask to join the Division of Crime Control of the Missouri State Highway Patrol. I did and was accepted. Now, my job was to look as rough, dirty, and villainous as possible, while the state of Missouri paid me to drink beer with these people that I would be arresting a few months later. Life was great.

About that time I met a guy who would influence my life greatly named Bill Silliman. Bill owned property and was an entrepreneur that had done very well. He was 70 years old, and I was 22, but it was an instant friendship. Bill knew how to make money, and I listened to every word he said as if it were the gospel. Bill and I were nearly inseparable over the next few years, buying and selling everything from cars to Beanie Babies.

Bill and his business partner, Elmer Battles, owned a 9-acre lot of commercial property that sat directly behind the house that I had just constructed. That 9-acre lot was at an intersection of highways –- U.S. Highway 60 and Missouri Route AD – a spot where the traffic count was astonishing. The only problem was, there was nothing around yet, other than my house and those highways.

Bill and Elmer came to me and offered me the property and suggested that Tina and I build a convenience store on it. I was 24 years old, never worked at a convenience store, and it seemed like the best idea I had ever heard. So, we did it. I went to the bank and asked for a half-million dollars to build it, and they gave it to me.

Before long, we had to decide between the Highway Patrol and our business. The business was hardly making any money, so the option to sell it was not viable. So, the real options were bankruptcy and stay on as a state trooper, or quit the highway patrol and work 24-hour days until we built our business to a stronger position.

We never considered filing bankruptcy, so I quit my dream job, and we worked. We worked, we worked, and we worked. Finally, after about three years of working, we realized that the business was better, and we started to accumulate money. So over the next few years we invested in real estate and other stores, and before long, we had one of the busiest small chains of convenience stores in Southeast Missouri.

After 11 years of doing this, we started to become complacent and a little bored, so we started looking for something else to do. In our search, we had found a small beach community in Florida where we vacationed that we absolutely fell in love with. I remember the first time we saw the Gulf of Mexico as we drove into the community. It was stunning! We rented a home on the little two-lane road known as Scenic County Road 30A.

As the community's newest residents, we fell further in love with this little section of heaven in Northwest Florida. There wasn't much traffic and true locals were few, but they were the nicest, most laid-back people I had ever met. The most prevalent vibe of the entire community was kindness. It was like a hidden, secret paradise. The crowds were limited to some holidays, key events, and a few weeks of summer. The beauty of the landscape, people, and weather was like a dream from which I didn't want to wake. Scenic 30A was our new dream and we wanted to move there badly. So, we searched for a way.

We heard of some others who were developing a new franchise model that involved sandwiches and cheesecakes. That's really all we knew about them, but never the less, we would end up being their first franchise location. We asked them about the business and it seemed like a perfect match.

Thinking back, Tina and I were probably spoiled with success. We thought that we could take anything and make it successful, no matter what it was. My belief then was if you work hard enough, it would work. I still believe this, but my lack of due diligence regarding this business opportunity would end up playing a huge role in our financial downfall.

I CAN AND I WILL

CHAPTER TWO
THE MOVE

We sold our businesses, office, houses, inventory, and all other assets to move to Florida and start this business. We found a little spot near the 30A area, leased a building, and bought a home. How could life be any better than this? Everything seemed so perfect. I still remember the smell of the air at night as I stood outside looking to the sky.

Something wasn't right though. I felt uneasy and looking back, I should have seen the storm coming. Not long after we moved, I could feel problems that we never anticipated.

I remember thinking many nights, "if I could just talk with my Dad, he would know what to do". He was the only person in our lives that would always tell us the truth. He would give advice, and I would always listen. Sometimes, I cussed, yelled and told Tina how his advice was stupid and it wasn't right, but I was always smart enough to listen to him, and every time, he was right. He died a few years before this and my rock of advice and my best friend was gone. Now, I didn't have him to go to and I was lost.

I had underestimated the immediate halt of income, and I never anticipated the crash of the economy that was about to take place. However, I still felt somewhat comfortable because there were several unfinished sales of property in Missouri, and we could, at least, pay our creditors and still have a little left to live on after we got here.

The business was built, and a few people came, but not many. The product was not good. The franchise we purchased was selling cakes made with Duncan Hines cake mix and frozen cookies. The cheesecakes were made in Missouri and shipped frozen to us and they were usually damaged. This area of Florida was filled with world-renowned chefs. Duncan Hines cakes and frozen cookies did not meet the standard the people, although kind and generous, were used to.

Then making things worse, the economy crashed and people stopped vacationing at our little beach community. It wasn't long until we couldn't keep up with our bills. A few days later, a large truck pulled up to our business, backed up to the door and loaded up all our equipment. It was the franchisor and apparently there was a loophole in the contract that allowed them to do this. They had official-looking documents, so I let them take it. We were just tired. We didn't' have it in us to even try to defend ourselves, so, we sat back and watched these people load up hundreds of thousands of dollars in equipment and drive off. They even took personal things such as phone chargers, ladders, pictures, and family items I can never replace. It was so strange, though, somehow, I felt like everything was okay.

Now, with no business, all our money spent on the move and the franchise, things started a fast downward swirl. We still had a few rays of hope as there were some people who owed us a lot of money, and at least, we could collect from them, pay our debts, and have a fresh start, and our dignity. Sadly, the people who owed us money stopped returning my phone calls and we couldn't collect.

When evil people know that you're broke and cannot defend yourself, they take advantage. In a time when we needed help, they stopped paying and even stole the things we couldn't get back home to get. Our house was days from foreclosure when we had one last chance.

We had sold our home in Missouri and the family we sold it to had leased it with the balance due at the end of the lease. Thank God! That date was approaching in a few days. I called and the representative sent the papers for Tina and me to sign. I spoke with him regarding the sale and I still remember our conversation. He told me that he just wanted my family to get back on our feet and he wasn't charging anything for the paperwork. Just sign the documents and you'll have $17,000 in a few days. $17,000 was the money left after the mortgage was paid on the home.

Tina and I were so happy. This money would allow us to bring our home mortgage current, and we could start fresh, with jobs and begin to work on ways to pay our creditors. Things were finally looking up.

A few weeks passed and we never received any money. Meanwhile, our cars were repossessed and the home we lived in was foreclosed on. The papers we signed were for the transfer of property and not the sale of our home. I felt like I had let my family down, and at that moment, I didn't want to live any longer. Somehow, I had made a string of bad decisions, and when I had one last chance to make it right, I screwed this up too. I had trusted this man who told me to sign those papers.

But, I felt like Ricky and Tina needed me and there was a little part of me that kept hoping for good things. I felt like I owed it to them to get out of this mess.

We had an old borrowed car with nearly expired plates and a rotten convertible top. The car leaked oil, antifreeze and brake fluid, but this car would end up being a huge part of our lives for the next few weeks, as next, the Sheriff's Department posted an orange eviction notice on the front door of our home, giving us a few days to get out.

I remember thinking, "How could this be happening to us?" We were not drug addicts, we were not mentally ill, we had an education and we were intelligent people. How could we become homeless? Only those types of people were homeless, not us. How in the world could this be happening to us?

I knew I believed in God, but I wasn't raised in a church environment and only attended a handful of times in my life. Somehow, I could only think of one person to turn to and I had never turned to Him before.

I walked from my house to the beach and instinctively, I dropped to my knees and cried. That was weird because I had worried about my inability to cry in the past when I felt like I should have been crying at some funerals, or at many touching moments of my life, but could not. I had cried one time during my adult life, and it was at my dad's funeral, but here I am on a beach in Florida, all alone, and crying.

I asked God to forgive me for the horrible things I had done and I prayed a real prayer for the first time in my life, or at least I thought it was a real prayer. I prayed for my wife, my son, my brother, my mother and my wife's family.

I prayed for my friend, Don Garner.

I prayed for my physically handicapped friend, Harold Razor.

I prayed for the homeless and the mentally ill.

I prayed for police officers and firefighters.

I asked God to talk to my dad and tell him that I was sorry and to tell him that I missed him.

I asked God to please tell my friend, Winfred Garner, that I missed him.

Winfred was my friend who had died a few years before. I looked to Winfred for advice constantly and losing him was devastating, as I had lost a father figure. The last thing that I asked of God was to give me the wisdom, strength, and the ability to make Him proud. And, I also asked Him to give me the wisdom, strength, and ability to make my wife, son and dad proud.

Thinking back, I'm not sure why I selected some people to pray for and left some out, but those were the people that I thought about that day. I wish I could tell you there was some type of loud theatrical voice that answered my prayers immediately, but there was not. But, I do remember that when I knelt, the waves were crashing onto the shore loudly, but after I started praying, there was total silence. The waves stopped. The sounds of the seagulls stopped and there seemed to be nothing on that beach at that moment except God and me.

As I prayed, I realized that it was not the end until I quit, or God says it's the end. Now, for me to give up seemed to be an insult to the amazing gift of life He had given me. It wasn't the end yet, and now I realized that.

As soon as I stopped praying, something told me that I had the wisdom, strength, and ability to do all the things that I had asked for. A complete renewal of my soul had just occurred on that beach in Florida. Wow. I get chills every time I relive that day.

I walked back to my foreclosed-on home with absolutely no clue what to do, but I had all the answers I needed. My story wasn't over, so I was not quitting now.

Although I had the answers I needed, the road to get back on our feet was not so simple. When we have the answers we're looking for, we must take action for those problems to be solved. These answers were simple, but not easy. It would take dedication, perseverance, love, hard work and faith in God and His word to get through this. If I was looking for easy, it wasn't there, but I was now prepared for the battle with these circumstances and ready to make it right.

It's difficult to explain the feeling of peace after I gave my life to Jesus Christ. I knew the problem was going to be taken care of, somehow. Miracles were nearly non-existent before this, but after, they became common. I'll talk about these miracles throughout this book, but one thing you'll need to notice is that although miracles were abundant after this day, they didn't happen without effort. I truly believe that even God wants us to honor Him and His blessings by using the gifts and ability He gave us to receive those blessings He desperately wants us to have.

Tina and I decided to tell our son, Ricky, that we were taking care of a few business-related issues and he stayed with some of his friends. We knew that he was aware of the situation, as he was at the house with his friends when the police posted an eviction notice on our door. We also knew that we had to get out of the house and we didn't want anyone to know what was going on. Hopefully, this would only be for one night, and we would work out something with the bank, and there wouldn't be too many questions asked.

It was not that difficult to keep our problems a secret because, as soon as the financial difficulties began, not many family members or friends called anymore. I know they still loved us, but it was like we had a contagious disease to which they couldn't help, and to an extent, they were right. Nobody knew the extreme nature of our financial woes, because it seemed to all happen overnight. Our families were poor, so there was absolutely nothing they could do for us and we didn't want to worry them.

CHAPTER THREE
WHAT DO WE DO NOW?

We packed few things in the car and intended to camp at a local campground until we figured out where to go. Only one problem, those campgrounds were expensive and we didn't have money.

We drove to a beach access and found a parking spot away from the main entrance where we settled in and talked for a while. We took a long walk on the beach, talked more, and found a place to sit down. We sat there for hours until a storm starting brewing in the Gulf.

Tina and I walked back to the car and counted our money, which didn't take long. We had $19.70. A few months before, we had hundreds of thousands of dollars and now we had $19.70. It started raining and we talked more about what we needed to do to get out of this mess we were in. We had been extremely disgusted with the franchise we invested in because nothing was home-made. Tina had decided that we needed to find those old family recipes that were tucked away and make them even better. Fresh, home- made cakes and cupcakes perfected and sold from a cupcake truck was our business plan. It sounds like the business plan of a 10- year-old little girl, but somehow it made perfect sense that night.

Then, all the sudden, the rain began to come inside the car like a waterfall coming through the roof. Tina and I scooted toward the center of the car, holding onto each other tight. You could almost feel the wheels of our minds creating our little bakery as we were getting rained on.

I was scared, but it wasn't the sound of thunder or the flashing of the lightening that scared me. Here's a guy that was a lifelong police officer, not scared of anything, sitting in a borrowed car, homeless and trying to keep from crying in front of his wife. It was the uncertainty and knowing that we didn't have a home to go to. It was the desperate feeling of inadequacy because we had to send our son to his friend's houses as we tried to figure out what to do.

As terrified as we were that night, I still remember the smell of an overheated car and motor oil, but mostly, the aroma of a fresh rain that was overwhelmingly calming. It's so funny how God can send something to you in a time of need. It can be something so simple as the smell of a summer rain. That aroma taught me to look for the silver linings in every situation.

I learned that night to take those miracles of nature God had supplied us all with and use them to meditate and ease the pain or confusion for a moment until the answer was supplied to me. I used that lesson to train my mind to take any situation and strain the bad from it focusing only on the positive. Now, sometimes I had to get extremely creative to find the good during situations, but it was always there. Not one time did good not show up. The rain coming inside that old car would have been a devastating blow but I focused on the beautiful aroma of the summer rain and everything else went away for a moment.

We knew that we couldn't go from never having baked a cake from scratch to making a living doing this any time soon, but that seed was planted that first night of homelessness. The old me would have simply forfeited to a life of labor for survival until I died, but now I knew my life had a purpose, and the obstacles I was hurdling were temporary. They were making me stronger for my new life with a purpose. I also realized that how in the world could a crazy idea like this, planted into our minds at such a dire time be wrong? Even though we wouldn't open the bakery for a couple of years, the business was born that night, in that old car, during that storm. If we didn't follow through with this, it would be like telling God that He was wrong and we couldn't do that.

We had been cleaning houses and one of our clients owed us for a few houses we had already completed, so we decided to try to sleep and then go collect that money the following morning. We dozed off a few times during the night and the storm subsided around 4 a.m.

We took another walk and watched the sun rise over the Gulf of Mexico. If you've never seen this, put it on your bucket list. We looked at each other and said at the exact same time, "we made it". It may have been the longest night of our lives, but we made it through together. At that moment, I had a shred of hope that if Tina and I stuck together, we'd make it through this somehow.

My entire life I had strived for more, and more, and more. Now, there was a strange peaceful feeling in connection with being completely broke. As devastating as it was, I now felt like, with God, I could tackle the world, and that weight of the old world was removed from my shoulders. I knew everything was going to be okay. But little did we know that wouldn't be our only night to sleep in that old car.

I CAN AND I WILL

CHAPTER FOUR
LET'S MOW A YARD!

The sun was shining and we had a new day. It was like we had just completed a marathon. We were exhausted, but so excited to see the sunshine and the feeling of accomplishment was overwhelmingly exhilarating. But before we could do anything, first, we needed to get gasoline and oil for the car.

I still remember being embarrassed to buy $5 worth of gas, but that was about 25 percent of all the money we had. Now, we had to spend another $3 on a quart of oil. Next on the list, we drove to collect the money owed to us for cleaning those homes. We drove to Seaside and the lady was not at home.

Down to about $11, hungry, worried about our son, and not sure what to do about it was a frightening feeling. Tina and I started looking around as we drove. We were looking for work, any work. As we were driving down 30A, we noticed a really nice home with a "for sale" sign in the yard with grass that was extremely tall.

Surprisingly, our cell phones were only disconnected for a couple of days at a time, so we had service during the entire 10 days we were homeless. So, we called the real estate agent whose number was on the sign and asked if we could mow the yard for $75 and he said "yes." I have no idea where we came up with charging $75 as I think I had become oblivious to people's earnings over the last decade of success, but $75 must have been a cheap price, because he immediately agreed to it.

We were so excited at the prospect of having money that we forgot that we didn't have a lawn mower, so, we borrowed a push mower from a friend and started to work. In mowing that yard, I realized quickly that people providing lawn services for others earned their money. We didn't have a weed eater either, so we had to pull all the weeds by hand. Nine hours later we were finished, and tired. Boy, was that a long day. But when the real estate agent met us at the house and paid us the $75, there was another feeling of accomplishment that kept us going. We figured it out again.

It was getting dark and the sun going down was a reminder that another night was about to be upon us. It's funny how the sun was now a feeling of security, and night-time was terrifying.
We called and checked on Ricky, as we would every day for the next 10 days and then prepared for another night in that old car.

We felt more comfortable staying at the same beach access as we did the night before, but this time, a new adventure was upon us. We were both filthy dirty and needed to bathe. You don't think much about this when you have a home. I took my shower and toilet for granted and I didn't understand the blessing those simple items were in my life.

We had some toiletries in a bag with us and around midnight, washed off under an outside shower at the beach then changed into some clean clothes and settled in for another long night. For a couple of people who had spent the last 15 years of our lives staying at swanky hotels and living in expensive homes, it was not easy to brush our teeth in a public restroom. I tried to look at it as an adventure that we were not forced into, but something we were doing by choice, kind of like being on the reality show, "Survivor," which helped.

I had also trained myself to believe that everyone was going through difficult times, and to a certain degree, many people were experiencing financial problems in our area, just not like ours. Not many people in our area were homeless, and we didn't want anyone to know about our situation.

Night 2 in the old car was a little different. We were in a better

18

financial situation because we had more than $50 now, and as that may seem minuscule, but considering the night before, we had nearly tripled our assets in one day.

We filled gallon jugs with water while mowing the yard earlier, so we stayed hydrated, but had forgotten to eat. So, we walked to a Tom Thumb Convenience Store and bought two Lunchable Snack Packs, sat on the beach and had dinner after midnight. Emotions were running much higher on night 2, as we both went from being frightened to being angry.

For some reason, no matter how illogical our reasoning was, we felt like people should be calling and begging to help us. We had helped a lot of people over the years, so all the good we had done should be returned to us since we were in need now, right? We bought thousands of bottles of water for Hurricane Katrina victims. We helped our family financially. We donated money to almost anyone that had asked us to for the past 10 years. If anyone needed a vehicle, I loaned it to them. Where is everyone now?! My phone was ringing every 10 minutes when I had money, and now it wasn't ringing at all.

Reflecting back, I think, how selfish this way of thinking is. God didn't intend for us to do good things with the expectation of being repaid. If I expected a return on my good deeds, it was never truly "doing good". So, maybe everything I had done wasn't good, and it was just us being selfish and expecting a return later in life, in case I needed these people.

I was that guy who thought I was good, but I wasn't. This was a conclusion that I didn't come to quite yet, but I was getting there.

After we ate our dinners, we talked more and went to sleep angry at everyone, but each other. We were placing blame and finding reasons to be mad at everyone but us. The only good that came after midnight of night 2 was we still were not mad at each other, just at the rest of the world. We were also still somewhat optimistic, because we thought, again, that this would be our last night sleeping in a car. Again, this optimism would be replaced with reality the following day.

CHAPTER FIVE
PHONE BILL DUE?

Day 3 was upon us and we both felt good about it. If we could collect for those houses we cleaned, we would have $400 added to our money. We drove back to Seaside and picked up a check for $400. Another accomplishment! Again, moments like this were what kept us going.

During this entire ordeal, Tina and I always acted so proud, and never wanted anyone to see the struggles we were going through. The lady who was paying us asked if she could run upstairs and get a check. I acted like it was nothing, and if today was a bad day, we'd come back tomorrow while in reality, that $400 was nearly everything to us.

The woman gave us two more houses to clean. These houses were in extremely nice neighborhoods. I'm not sure why, but Tina and I were both embarrassed and we didn't want anyone to know that we were cleaning houses. The houses we cleaned were vacation rentals, which meant that nobody would be in the house while we cleaned, but arriving after. So, if we could just get inside that home without anyone seeing us carrying cleaning supplies, nobody would know that we were the "cleaning crew".

We went to a beach supply store and bought four cloth bags, for $2 each to put our cleaning supplies in so that we would look like tourists going inside our home that we had rented for the weekend. After we got inside, we worked, and worked hard. If being a Missouri State Trooper taught me anything, while at the academy, they taught me how to clean well. We'd have to clean our rooms while there with a fine-toothed comb and if we didn't, the instructors would yell, scream, and believably threaten to kill us within an inch of our lives. So, I was a damned good cleaner!

We collected our pay for these two houses and had another $200 to add to our cash. Day 3 was one of the best days of our lives. We had less than $80 when we woke up and now, more than $600!

We called to check on Ricky. He was fine, and we gave him $100. This situation had to be so difficult for him. A few weeks before, he was driving to a new school in a new car, and now suddenly, he was either being driven to school in an old broken- down car, walking, or trying to find a way to get there with a friend. If being a teenager wasn't hard enough, this didn't help. Tina and I were raised poor, so being broke was nothing new, but sudden. In Ricky's case, he had never been through anything like this and he didn't deserve it. He did nothing to make this happen. I had to make this better and I had to do it quickly!

Tina and I decided that we were going to spend some of our money on a cheap hotel for the night, so we could clean ourselves up, rest, and tackle Day 4 energized and ready. We had enough money to do this, or so we thought.

But before we could find time to locate a hotel at which to stay for the night, we received a text that said our phone would be shut off if the bill wasn't paid before midnight. We were behind on the bill, so the amount due was more than $300. The logical thing to do would seem to be to let the phone be shut off and get a hotel. The only problem was that this was our lifeline of communication with Ricky.

Again, God had blessed us, because if we'd have received that text one day earlier, we would not have had the money to pay the bill. We had to be able to contact him and his phone was included on this account. The decision was easy. We paid the bill and prepared for another night in that old car.

Day 3 was still a success, and we were moving forward. We had a fancy dinner at McDonalds and went right back to our beach-access parking lot.

Some of my favorite moments in life now are having dinner with my wife. During those 10 days, that was the time we formulated a plan, and it always seemed to be such an optimistic time of the day. Those ideas we ran by each other, and dreams we shared over a burger helped to keep us motivated and looking forward to tackling the next obstacle. It's a much different circumstance now, but our dinners are still, basically, the same thing. We talk about what's next, reflect, and it's still one of the most optimistic times of my day.

I was getting comfortable with our beach-access parking spot and although we had only been there for three nights, it felt like a lot longer. It wasn't nearly as scary now, but something else scared me to death. I can see where people get used to being poor and that way of life becomes normal. That acceptance horrified me. I had to fight to not let this become the new life I fell into. I didn't want to make being unclean and wearing dirty clothes the new normal, so it was important to keep our clothes clean and not to look homeless.

This is not easy when you don't have a place to bathe or a washer and dryer to clean your clothes. I had to stay focused on getting my winning mentality back and this time of my life could not define me. It could not be the way I end my time that God has blessed me with.

The things you take for granted, like a washer and a dryer, a bed, your own bathroom, and a television were suddenly luxuries that we didn't have. We never looked homeless and I'm so proud of that. We washed our clothes when we cleaned houses. Tina started cutting my hair and I figured out how to shave, even if it was in a public restroom. It was important to me that we maintain our dignity and looking homeless was not an option. I felt like if we ever fell into that trap where we looked the part, we could never dig our way out.

We took a walk that evening before we tried to rest and walked by these homes that were worth millions of dollars. We picked out the ones we liked the most and talked about the one we wanted when we got back on our feet. What's strange is that at no point of this conversation did it feel like a dream. I truly felt like we could and would achieve success again. Now, my opinion of success may change, but that's for later.

We laughed a little more than the night before and talked about the things we missed. Although this was only our third night, we felt like we had been at this beach access for a decade.

I asked Tina what sucked the most about being poor. She said bar soap. I laughed and she asked me, "What about you?" I said, "Sharing deodorant with my wife".

We went back and forth with this conversation for about 30 minutes. Some of the things that sucked were, losing friends, cheap after-shave lotion, no water, no Diet Coke, no air conditioning, no electricity, getting clothes at Goodwill, not being able to donate to Goodwill, having to borrow, not being able to loan, asking for help, selling my golf clubs, cleaning houses for a living, not having a home of our own to clean, not being able to pay what we owe, my wife giving me haircuts, no health care, calluses, 1-800 numbers calling, mowing a yard for money, and lastly, not having your own yard to mow.

I know some of these are selfish, and there are many other things that most people would list, but for some reason, these are the ones we thought about, and some were simply to laugh about. I knew that it was my duty to laugh and to make Tina laugh. If I couldn't find a way to do this, we'd never survive.

We fell asleep a little after this conversation. It seems like that laughter made us sleep as soundly as possible with our feet on the dash and our heads in the back storage area of this two-seater car.

CHAPTER SIX
WE GOT NEW BIKES!

Day 4 started with a police car circling the parking lot at 5 a.m. Luckily, there were a couple of other cars on the lot that were there to see the sun rise.

But, this presented a problem for us that we really hadn't thought about. We had a car that wasn't ours. We had license plates on the car that expired the next day, and the biggest problem was that we couldn't just go and renew the license plates because those plates didn't belong to this vehicle. We had taken them off one of our cars that was repossessed and put them on this car. Gosh, what do we do now?

We had talked about buying a decent bicycle to ride to work when we didn't have gas or if one of us had to go one way while the other went a different direction. My inner-criminal came up with the idea of buying a bike and hanging the bicycle on the back of the car, which would block the view of the expired license plate. This would solve two problems with one small purchase. Now, we just had to find a bike, and around Florida, bikes are not cheap.

We looked on Craigslist, where a Cannondale bicycle was listed for $125, so we drove to find it. When we arrived, the guy had tons of bikes. He sold us two for $125 and, as if God was in on the conspiracy to hide my expired, illegal license plates, the guy threw in a trunk rack that fit that old car perfectly. We happily hung our two new bikes up, and just as planned, those bikes completely blocked the visibility of the license plates. Problem solved!

As that purchase took a large portion of our money, we needed to figure out how to make more of it fast. But, first, we acted like kids with new toys and rode our new bikes down 30A.

As we rode our bicycles, looking out at the Gulf, I remember thinking that none of this seemed real and I would be waking up soon from a horrible dream. Then I thought, look at what God has given me: my beautiful wife, my beautiful son, and this beautiful Gulf of Mexico to be with every day. So, I rode 10 miles thinking of how blessed I had been and realized that things could be much worse.

Somehow, I knew by this point that I'd be telling this story someday, and I wanted to make sure it had a happy ending. I had also realized by this point that it was up to me if this story ended happily and nobody else. Me, with the wisdom, courage, and word of God to follow would allow my family and me to get out of this.

We rode back to our parked car, hung our bikes back on the trunk and off we went to find our parking spot (home) for the night. We decided to go back to our same parking place. We were becoming disturbingly comfortable with our new home. Just as trying to keep our hygiene and clothes clean, we needed to get out of this car!

I wasn't as worried when we pulled into the parking lot. Again, this concerned me. If we became too comfortable with the situation we were in, would it become our new way of life? Was this parking lot becoming okay with me? I can see how this happens to people before they realize it.

The only thing we could do to make immediate money was to clean more houses. We had a house to clean in Seaside the next morning, so we talked about how to increase our business and marketing ideas.

We were homeless, broke, and excited about cleaning houses. In my mind then, I could see myself owning a house-cleaning empire and that kept my emotions up and gave me hope. If you think about it, that's all that keeps us going: hope. Whether we were cleaning houses, having yard-sales, running convenience stores, or mowing yards, we were going to act like we were entrepreneurs making money and living our dream. That state of mind kept us motivated and kept that hope we so desperately needed, alive.

We napped a few hours and awoke at 3 a.m. We were a little nervous that the police would drive back through the parking lot, so we decided to leave and go to Waffle House for breakfast. It was there we formulated a plan for Day 5.

I CAN AND I WILL

CHAPTER SEVEN
WALKING IN SEASIDE

We noticed that every house in Seaside had a picket fence with the name of the owner and the owner's home city painted on it. We decided to walk every street in town and write down the names of every owner in a notebook. We would then send a postcard to every one of these people offering our cleaning service, or whatever else they needed. We created some cheap postcards, sent them to those names we had gathered, and hoped for a couple of responses.

It seemed that every one of these ideas we would have would always give us a burst of energy when we were down. I noticed this, so my mind was constantly working, thinking of how to get out of this mess. We left Waffle House and headed out to clean.

As we were leaving the house we had to clean that day, a neighbor said they saw us cleaning homes around town and asked if we could stop and take care of her cat daily for the next two weeks because she and her family were leaving town. I'm not sure anyone had ever been so excited to empty a litter box daily than Tina and I were at that moment. She paid us $100 right then, so we were even more excited.

Little victories like this had to be sent by God. Who in their right mind, gives a key to their home to a couple of strangers, in an old worn-out car and asks them to go into their home to care for their beloved feline? Not only did we empty the litter box and check on the cat for the next couple of weeks, we vacuumed the floors and swept the area where the litter box was located. I'm not sure why we did this because we were not asked to. It may have something to do with the comfort of air conditioning. The woman was so pleased when she got back that we were tipped $20 for our efforts. She said she had never left the house with a cat sitter and come back to her house cleaner than it was when she left.

Occasionally people tipped when they were happy with our house cleaning, and those tips bought our food on many days. I've never forgotten what those tips meant to my family. I tip all service workers generously now, even when I really don't have the money to do it. I can assure you that if someone is a waitress, waiter, cleaning houses, or any other industry that provides a service to consumers, they can use the tip money, and most likely depend on it to survive.

We collected the money for cleaning the house, so Day 5 was becoming a wonderful day. Another little victory provided by God, and those successes kept us going. We were figuring out that if we kept moving forward that this was going to work out. We had to keep a positive attitude and we had to stay focused on success and not to get caught up in how we got in this situation.

It's weird, we hardly ever spoke of our situation or the things that happened to us. We hardly ever spoke of anything bad and avoided

30

wasting any of our energy on negative thoughts. We talked about good things. We spoke of what we were going to do when we got out of this situation. It was never a question of if, but when.

We figured out that if we kept throwing tons of prospective ideas out, when the occasional one would pay off, that was what we were living for. That feeling of inching our way toward getting out of that car was enough motivation to keep us forging ahead. We had to toss the failed ones aside and not even talk about them, kind of like they never even existed, and just talk about the ones that were successful. No matter how insignificant some victories were, we needed those wins. It was working, so we had to keep doing this!

Living from a car in Florida was not cheap. Our money was not accumulating as fast as you would think. Gas, oil, fast food, phones, post cards and stamps took a lot of the money we had coming in. We needed to do better, so we were depending on these post cards to pay off.

We drove up and down 30A searching for a new spot to park our car. We were becoming uneasy in our little spot we had felt so comfortable at for the last few nights. We decided to drive to Destin and park in a store's parking lot as we felt like we'd blend in better.

As we started nearly every night, we walked. We kept walking, avoiding that dreaded entry into that dreadful, uncomfortable car. Remembering back, and it even makes more sense now, that walking together strengthens relationships.

My father and I had become extremely close while I was in my early 20s. The reason for that bond was that we walked every day. We walked around 5 miles a day and talked the entire time. We talked about things that I still think about daily. We talked about things that he and I will be the only ones to ever know about. It was during this time of our lives that we became friends. I have absolutely no doubt that if he had been alive, this horrific situation we were in would have never happened. He would have been in Florida with us and we would have formulated a plan to make it, but without him, I couldn't do it.

Although Tina and I had been together since we were babies, I could feel a tighter bond between us after this time in our lives and those nightly walks gave us time to talk and become even closer. We walked back to the car and tried to rest for a few hours before taking on Day 6. But, we couldn't.

So we walked to Sonic and ordered a grilled-cheese sandwich to take back to the car for dinner. I went to a vending machine to get a soda and Tina got into the car with our food. When I got back to the car, I remember the aroma of that hot grilled cheese was spectacular and overwhelmingly strong inside that car. As we sat and ate, I had a light bulb turn on in my mind! If I could come up with some type of idea that made a home smell as strong with an aroma as that grilled cheese smelled, we could be rich! Thinking back now, I'm sure I was just hungry and that grilled cheese was the best I had ever eaten, or so it seemed.

We walked into Wal-Mart and bought a bag of lava rocks and a pint of fresh linen fragranced oil. We also bought a cake baking pan to place the lava rocks in. The plan was to pour the oil onto the lava rocks and let them soak. You would then place the rocks into an oven and bake at a low temperature while the concoction heated up and spread a magnificent fragrance throughout the home. We were going to try our new creation the following morning while we cleaned that 2-million-dollar home. In our minds, we had the perfect invention that would be a must-have for every home across the United States. Our problems were solved! Little things like this, as silly as they may seem now, were what kept us going too. We were ready to bathe, shave and get some rest to take on Day 6.

One good thing about living in a tourist-based beach area, there are many public restrooms, and it wasn't that difficult to wash up, and even shave when it wasn't busy. We figured out very quickly that even though it was only a few miles down the road from our 30A home, it was not home.

From the moment we pulled onto 30A while on vacation more than five years before all of this happened, I knew this was where God wanted me to be. I can't explain it, but a feeling of peace and comfort was there, even if we were sleeping in our car. So we didn't get any sleep that night and drove back to our safe place, 30A.

I CAN AND I WILL

CHAPTER EIGHT
LAVA ROCKS A BURNING

Day 6, here we come! We drove to our house to clean, and took our treasured answer-to-everything lava rocks in with us. The real estate agent had called to tell us about a home showing that morning, as this extravagant house was on the market to sell. This was even more perfect. We would place the new invention inside the oven to heat as the rise in temperature would increase the aroma of the lava rocks while we were cleaning, and whenever the potential home buyer arrived, they would be overwhelmed with this magnificent, fresh linen aroma, then immediately purchase the house.

Just as many things in our lives, this didn't go as planned either. We were so busy cleaning that we forgot about the fragranced rocks in the oven. When the real-estate agent stopped by to make sure everything was perfect in the house, she instead noticed smoke rolling from the oven.

She screamed "Are you cooking something? It's burning! It's burning cookies!". I ran to the oven and took the lava rocks to the exterior deck as black smoke rolled from them. The smell of burned lava rocks filled this multi-million-dollar home. We finished cleaning and left as quickly as possible. As badly as I felt about this, the things that had happened to us had changed me. It wasn't the end of the world and maybe it was because our life had created a mentally unstable couple, we said as we laughed. The more we talked about it, the more we laughed. We still talk about that day, and we still laugh like it just happened.

Day 6 was not going so great, and little did we know that it would get worse. Even though we had nearly burned a house down, the real estate agent asked us if we could clean another home. We jumped at the opportunity to make $90 more.

We arrived at this house, and it was in an extremely nice neighborhood, but a little older than the other houses. We walked in and looked at each other in disbelief. It was a disaster. There was trash everywhere. I've never seen so much wet, black hair in bathroom sinks, toilets, showers, bathtubs, and the floor. It's one thing to clean your own bathroom and yours or your children's hair from a sink or floor, but it's disgusting to clean other people's. This was not easy for me to get used to, but there wasn't a choice, at that moment. I had to do it.

The kitchen was littered with food and it appeared as if the trash hadn't been taken out for days. The smell was disgusting. As I was cleaning the soiled toilet with rubber gloves on, my phone rang. My phone didn't ring much anymore, unless it was a bill collector, and I never answered. This was a local number and didn't appear to be a business, so after the second attempt, I took my gloves off and answered.

It was a credit card company trying to collect money that I owed. I tried to explain the situation that we were in and that we were trying our best to get back on our feet. He told me that they were going to initiate a garnishment on my pay and I explained again, but never told him that we were homeless. It's so weird, I was embarrassed to tell a bill collector that we were sleeping in a car. Finally, he asked for a current mailing address because the bills they were sending were being returned. I told him that we were "in between" places to stay.

For some reason, that felt like a better choice of words. He laughed. That laugh made me absolutely furious. I'm not sure why it triggered the tirade that I unleashed on this guy, but I may be the only person in history that a bill collector hung up on. I wanted to call him back and finish my rant, but I didn't.

We worked another eight hours cleaning that house. That may have been the hardest money we'd ever earned, as we were paid $45

36

each for nearly 10 hours of work, but we were proud to get it. That was $90 we didn't have before and many times, people stay idle because they would rather do nothing than to work for a small amount of money. Although we may have complained to each other, we were extremely grateful for the work. It was late and we had one more house to clean in Santa Rosa Beach.

We were absolutely exhausted when we arrived at this house and it was after dark. We hurriedly worked our way through the dirty home and had finished everything but taking out the trash. I ran upstairs to get the trash while Tina grabbed the bag in the downstairs bathroom. I heard her scream, and ran back downstairs as quickly as I could. She was holding her hand tightly and showed me her injury. It was a small spot on her finger that was bleeding. Nothing that looked like it should be of any concern. But when she showed me what caused it, I was scared to death. It was a hypodermic needle left in the trash that broke her skin.

I had no idea what to do. We had no health insurance and barely had enough money to put gasoline in our vehicle for the next day. In most cases, I'm the calm personality, and Tina is the one who overreacts. Here, I was not calm. As a former member of the Division of Drug and Crime Control with the Missouri State Highway Patrol, I knew the types of people who left uncovered needles inside trash cans. Most likely, the needle was for drug use, and we all know the diseases that these drug addicts could have been infected with.

I called the owner of the home and he was equally as panicked as I was. He contacted the renter of the house, who assured him that the needle was being used to inject insulin as he was a diabetic. The owner assured us that he believed this man, as he was an older, and a seemingly level-headed senior, to which I replied, no level-headed person leaves a needle uncapped inside a trash can for someone else to pick up! We felt like, with the owner's assurance, that everything was okay and left there nervous, but in good faith that all was going to be alright, and it was.

It was late and we were off to find another spot to spend the night. This was always the worst part of the day. Finding that place to park that old car was never easy. We didn't talk about it during the day. I guess we thought something would happen during the day and we wouldn't have to sleep in the car. It seems like we hadn't had time to worry about much, so staying busy was such a blessing.

I kept thinking that this nightmare was going to end soon and this hope helped me stay sane. I told myself that God was going to take care of us, and although I didn't know how we were going to make this better, I knew that He was going to when the time was right. He knew exactly what He was doing. Each of these experiences were needed to make me a better person. I learned from every trial that I faced and those lessons will guide me through the rest of my life.

Day 6 had been testing our faith. To make things worse, one of the headlights went out on the car, and you don't want to get pulled over for one headlight when you're hiding your expired plates with bicycles hanging on the trunk of someone else's car.

So, we stopped at WaterColor Resort and parked behind the condominiums. But, we couldn't sleep in the car because we would have been noticed and run off. So, we took a blanket to the beach and slept there. That night, we slept better than we had in a while. I felt like we were okay and the beach was a safe zone for us. I still get a feeling of peace when I'm on the beach, like nothing can hurt me there.

We woke up with the sunrise, and it may have been the most beautiful sunrise I've ever witnessed. That sunrise is my happy place. When I feel concerned or overwhelmed, I go there. What a wonderful way to start Day 7!

CHAPTER NINE
JUMPING HURDLES

That feeling didn't last long. Day 7 ended up being one that nearly destroyed us. Our car wouldn't start and we needed to get to two houses to clean. The radiator was leaking antifreeze/water and was empty.

We walked to a convenience store and purchased antifreeze. It seemed like the longest walk I'd ever been on. I had never thought much about transportation and the luxury of having it. I never thought about people that didn't have a car to get to work, and it never crossed my mind that anyone had to do this.

As Tina and I walked, I thought about this, but I don't remember being sad for us, but sad for others. It was almost like I was still in denial and hadn't accepted that I was poor and more than poor -- homeless.

It helped that there were always a lot of walkers on 30A, but Tina was self-conscience that people knew we were not walking for exercise because she was carrying her purse that day. She still hates to carry a purse if we walk anywhere, and we have a car now. I think it reminds her of days like this.

We got back to the car and poured the antifreeze in the radiator and watched it drain straight onto the asphalt. We still hadn't solved the problem and had two houses to clean with no transportation. There was only one thing to do. Tina would ride her bike to one of the homes and I would ride to the other. It wasn't an ideal situation, but there were enough cleaning supplies at those two houses that we could make it work without taking anything with us on the bikes.

It was a strange feeling. We had hardly been apart since all this had happened and as I rode off on my bicycle, I felt completely lost without her. I worried that she felt the same way. Tina had to ride about four miles one way and I rode about the same in the other direction. Somehow, we got the houses cleaned and met back at our car before dark, but the sun was going to set soon.

I figured out where the radiator was leaking, but had no idea how to repair it. If anyone knows anything about me, it would be that I'm no mechanic. I had never changed a flat tire in my life, much less fixed a leaking radiator, but I had an idea.

There were two tubes of JB Weld in the trunk. For those of you who don't know what JB Weld is, I'm not sure either, but it looked like some type of miracle super glue. The name of this glue seemed to indicate that it may be as good as welding something, so maybe it was the perfect product for my problem. The idea was to let the radiator dry, put the JB Weld on the spot that was leaking, and it would fix our problem.

We were both exhausted from cleaning, walking, and riding, so we found a cheap dinner and tried to get some rest. I knew that night that we had to figure something out soon. Our bodies and minds couldn't keep doing this.

I know that God had to be with us because anyone would have lost hope/faith by now, but we hadn't. We kept figuring out solutions to every problem that we were faced with. The only difference was that those little things that were funny weren't any more. Although we were working our way through every situation that was thrown at us, we were getting tired. Little did I know that there were a lot more hurdles to jump before we got out of that old car.

CHAPTER TEN
SHAME, LOVE, AND REALIZATION

Day 8 was upon us and it started with a victory. I fixed the car!

JB Weld worked and after another walk to the convenience store and more antifreeze, we were mobile once again. For a guy who had never fixed anything before in his life, this was a huge accomplishment. For a split second, I felt my calling might be working on cars, then I realized that I may not be able to repair everything with JB Weld, so, that dream was crushed.

Day 8 was filled with phone calls, and it was one of the worst days of my life. Some of our family members called and were asking about things they were hearing regarding homes being foreclosed on and court dates that involved the properties. I know they all love us but it was like they were looking for us to deny the rumors regarding the financial problems, and when we couldn't, the conversations were short.

Then, I received a call that there was someone at my mother's home, to repossess her vehicle. This was absolutely devastating to me. I had purchased a vehicle for her and it was included on one of the bank notes with a piece of property that I was losing. I had spoken to the bank regarding my mom's car and I had already turned over all our vehicles, but I thought I had worked out a plan to save my mother's car.

I knew that I couldn't pay. I was living from a borrowed car and had pennies to my name, but I kept thinking I could save this vehicle somehow. I couldn't. The complexity of the loan being tied to real estate made it impossible for her to take over the payments that I had been paying, so it was hopeless. There was nothing I could do and it devastated me.

Two more people called that day that I had always loaned money to when they needed it, asking for more money. I couldn't give them any, and that made me feel ashamed. They've never called me again since that day. Another called to borrow my vacation home in Branson, and I've never heard from them again either.

What had happened to me? I was the guy that people were depending on and now, I had nothing. For some reason I was embarrassed more than ever. There was no obligation for me to do many of the things that I had done over the years, but I felt like I was letting these people down. I had hidden the fact that we were homeless and still didn't share this information with the ones who called that day, including our families.

Day 8 crushed me and I wasn't sure that I could keep going on. Then my phone rings again and I considered not answering it, but I did. It was my best friend, Don Garner. The conversation was brief, and he had no idea that Tina and I had been living in a car for eight days. All he wanted was to know if I was okay. He asked that and told me that he loved me. He didn't want anything but that.

That phone call was exactly what I needed. Just to hear those words, "Are you okay?" and "I love you", wasn't heard much since we lost everything and the timing of Don's call couldn't have been better.

I needed to know that someone was concerned about Tina, Ricky and me, and not worried about a rumor, or not losing their personal bank, or concerned that my reputation had been tarnished by this set of events. That phone call may have saved my life. It definitely gave me the will to go clean some more houses and keep working to do better and helped me survive Day 8.

So we cleaned, and cleaned some more until it was almost midnight. We slept in the parking lot inside the gated community where we were cleaning the houses that day. I knew that Day 9 had to be better.

What made Day 8 so bad was having to come to the realization that we couldn't help others financially like we had for years. The day had been no different than the preceding seven days, other than the phone calls, so what made it so bad? I'd like to think that it was because I couldn't help the people that I'd always helped, but I'm not sure that was it. Was I helping others to inflate my ego, or was I helping for the right reason? I'm still not sure about this, maybe a little of one and a lot of the other.

I CAN AND I WILL

CHAPTER ELEVEN
HARD WORK, PRAYER, AND BELIEF

Day 9, I'm ready for anything, so bring it!

It felt like even though we were working extremely hard and faithful with our daily routine of survival, that we were still not doing something right. God was trying to tell us something else, but we were still blinded by the situation we were in and could not see everything He wanted us to see yet. It would take us another day, but we'd figure it out.

We had a condominium to clean in Rosemary Beach, so we headed off to work. For anyone who hasn't cleaned for a living, it's tough. It's not like cleaning your personal house. Most of the time, you have to work fast, and cleaning fees are charged ranging from a "normal" clean to a "deep" clean. As the words suggests, the deep clean is more intense and usually done once a year for vacation rental homes. The deep cleans would include things like cleaning under and behind furniture, window sills and baseboards, along with many other things.

This was the first time we had ever cleaned this home and the fee for a regular cleaning was $80. We worked for about five hours and headed to our next house, but stopped to grab lunch before starting.

About 9 p.m. our phone rang, just as we were finishing this last house of the day. Someone said, "Are you the cleaning lady?", to which Tina replied, "Yes".

I'm not sure why I was so offended by this question, but it still bothers me to this day. For this person that I've spent nearly my entire life with, and the epitome of class, eloquence and beauty to be referred to as the "cleaning lady" angered me.

It was a family from Atlanta calling that rented the condominium that we had cleaned earlier that day. They were not happy with the cleanliness of the house, so we hurried back to fix whatever was the problem.

We arrived around 9:30 p.m. and they pointed out a few things they felt needed attention. I told them that since it was so late, we'd return the next morning to take care of everything on their list, but they wanted it done right then.

One thing that being homeless does is it humbles you. We could have refused to do what they asked, but what if we didn't have these houses to clean? What would we do then?

The Atlanta people's list included cleaning under the couch, scrubbing the mini-blinds, cleaning under the refrigerator, and the glass patio doors on the outside deck. To make it worse, the lady and her mother stood with us while we worked. The daughter stayed with Tina and the mother with me. I could hear Tina being directed to do things, as the mother told me each item to clean. It seemed like it took me an hour to clean one mini-blind.

Thinking back, I get a little agitated about how they treated us, but I wasn't mad that night. I felt like a prisoner being ordered by a guard. What could be worse than this? The only option was to call someone and ask for money, then take that money and go back to Missouri and ask to live in one of our parent's homes.

I'm sure they would have been fine with it, but I was not going to do this. I already felt like I had disappointed everyone and I was not going to ask for anything. Tina and I had always figured out a way to succeed and we would get out of this too, but it better happen fast though because I couldn't stand being in this prison much longer.

It was almost midnight when we finished. I practically felt sorry for this family because they had spent nearly their entire first day in paradise supervising the cleaning crew. Now on to the last task of the day: find a place to sleep.

We were in Rosemary Beach, which was about 20 minutes from our normal beach access, and we were absolutely exhausted again. I didn't mention anything to Tina, but I was nervous, because we didn't have any homes to clean for the following day. We found a different beach access and parked for the night. It was an extremely quiet night, as we didn't discuss much of the day. It seems like Day 9 had sucked the life out of us. The last thought I had every night before and this one was no different, was to keep working hard, praying, and believing that things were going to work out, and they eventually would. We fell asleep and woke up to our last day of homelessness. Day 10!

I CAN AND I WILL

CHAPTER TWELVE
BE PERSISTENT, NOT DESPERATE

The phone rang early and it was a Seaside homeowner who resides in Atlanta. He had received our postcard regarding cleaning services and wanted to know if we could clean his house that day. What a wonderful blessing from God to start our day!

As we were cleaning that house, the phone rang again. A Seaside homeowner who lived in Memphis wanted her home cleaned that day also! Our postcards were paying off.

While we were cleaning one of these homes, a neighbor stopped us and asked if we could clean their home the following day.

I had been calling the bank that had served our eviction notice trying to work out a plan to stay for a few more days, but I could never work out an arrangement with whomever I was speaking. In Florida, houses were being foreclosed on at an alarmingly high rate, but most were vacation homes, not primary residences.

I thought that Day 10 started off so great and kept getting better, so I called the bank again and spoke with an extremely nice lady who seemed to actually listen to my story.

Even though I was homeless, I was speaking with confidence, and not desperation. Everything that we had been experiencing and working our way through had given me a boost of confidence that I had lost before. I believe now that desperation scares people away from helping you.

This lady told me that she might be able to help, but that she couldn't give me permission to go back to our house. However, I felt comfortable going back. She told me to check the house and if our key worked, go on in.

We finished cleaning those houses so fast, and drove directly to our old home. Our old key worked! You could tell that people had been inside, but everything was still there.

I called the mortgage company back because I felt like we could be arrested at any moment for burglary. I spoke with a different person who signed us up for a program to financially assist us if the house was cleared out, cleaned, and in great shape when we left. The final foreclosure would not occur for a few weeks, so we could stay until that happened.

When we got this news, it was around 2 p.m. We sat down on our couch, and didn't wake up until the following morning. Our 10 days sleeping in our car were over. Our problems were not solved, but we would not be driving up and down 30A looking for a beach access where we could park our car and sleep. This day was one of the best days of our lives!

CHAPTER THIRTEEN
AFTER THE 10 DAYS

A lot has happened since those 10 days of living in a borrowed car. Although we still have a long way to go, we are getting there.

We bought that cupcake truck we dreamed about during the first night we slept in that old car and created a thriving business that was extremely successful. In addition to selling our baked goods to locals and visitors who frequented the area's farmers' markets, we began selling our desserts to celebrities such as Emeril Lagasse, Zac Brown, Vern Yip, Mike Huckabee and many others. Vern was even kind enough to feature our cakes in his "Design Wise" book and we were invited to join him on "The Today Show" in New York City, which we did.

We published a successful cookbook based on our recipes we used from our families' archives, and we were blessed to be headlined in many local and national magazine articles. Our little cupcake truck became part of the Scenic 30A landscape and we were honored to be voted one of the Hot Spots on 30A for five years in a row. We were also selected as a "Perfect in South Walton" award winner.

Sweet Henrietta's Treats grew into a business that exceeded my wildest dreams. The business became so successful that we couldn't keep up with the demand, so we sold it and plan to spend the next year traveling and promoting this book based on our story, hoping to meet and help as many people as possible.

All the while we were growing our dessert business, I returned to school and earned another undergraduate degree in legal studies. I also finished my law degree.

Most importantly, though, Tina, Ricky, and I have a relationship with God that we didn't have before those 10 days of living in a borrowed vehicle.

Ricky plays in the church band and hardly misses a Sunday Service. All three of us learned that we can tackle anything that comes at us now. We took a bad situation and we made it a success story that we can't wait to share with everyone. We've come a long way since that rainy night in an old broken-down car.

I think about those 10 days a lot. Tina, Ricky and I instinctively did some things to survive that we didn't realize when they were happening. I think back and wonder why on Day 1 we didn't try to contact some type of social service program to get some assistance. Surely we would have qualified because we had $19.70 cents to our names and no place to live. It never crossed our minds to do this. I think all our energy was focused on how to get out of the situation, but we naturally knew only one way and that was to work.

We knew that we couldn't be choosy with our job selection because of the situation we had gotten ourselves into. The only job I had ever had was as a police officer and a business owner, and getting hired as a police officer was not logical when the police were serving eviction papers, all your transportation had been repossessed, and you were sleeping in an old car with the wrong license plates on it, and those license plates were expired.

How could we make money and make it at that moment, other than to ask for help? All we could come up with was cleaning houses. As this was a tourist-based economy, so there were always vacation rental homes to clean. If we were willing to do something that most people didn't want to do, and actually do it well, it was an immediate solution to our problem. It sucked, but I'm so proud of my family for doing this. At that time, I was ashamed and embarrassed, but now I'm not. Now, I am exploding with pride that my life had those 10 days, and those days have forever changed me.

I reflect on the decisions we made, most of them unknowingly, but instinctual. I believe that we all have these basic behavior patterns ingrained into our DNA by God, but we've let society change us. Somehow, over the past generation, we look for a problem to be solved by someone else, and even tend to blame others for our situation. My grandparents and great grandparents were self-sufficient and that entire generation was. My mother didn't have a car until she was 30 years old, so I remember many days, she would load my brother and me onto a bicycle to ride to the grocery store for food. Where has that work ethic gone today? If there wasn't food, they worked harder or made their own food.

Society is different now, and it's not because we let this happen out of hate or laziness. This happened by politicians trying to do good in the beginning. That good turned into dependence and has in turn created generations of people on social assistance who have no idea how to work themselves out of it.

Before we could get out of that car, we had to do a few things and I still apply these principles to my life today. To every situation I'm in, I scan my options internally, and then make my decision. It's kind of like a little conversation with God about everything.

These same principles can be applied to the situation you're in. It doesn't have to be as serious as the one I found myself in. You can take these same suggestions and work through a troubling time in a marriage. Just take them and apply them accordingly to your rough patch in life. Not every outcome will be like you want, but if you do these things, and perform them with your heart's desires, the situation will be solved by God, not you. As I said, that outcome will not always be what we want, and will hardly ever be as fast as we want, but it is what He knows is right. How can your decision be wrong when you have our Heavenly Father guiding you through the process?

Most self-help books tell you to formulate a detailed plan to succeed. This would not have worked for me, and I think a lot of people would be derailed from happiness and success if they do this. You must know where you are and what you want. Clarity of a detailed plan to get there may work for some, but it is not essential. In fact, I believe it could hinder the better life that God has in store for you.

These simple steps I took work and if you stay true to your faith, the reward is tremendous. Your course will always change. The world will not let you stick to a detailed plan, as it will continue to throw issues at you that you never thought would happen. If you let that kink in the plans stall your forward movement, you could fail, and never achieve that happiness and success we're all looking for.

Most people don't face homelessness, or completely being broke, but I believe that it was God's way of taking a guy that achieved success early and along with that success came an attitude of better than others, and greed. I had to go through this to change. Although

I was scared the entire time, it was like I had a new friend.

I know God had been talking to me my entire life, but once you get that mindset of thinking you have all the answers, you don't listen to what He is saying. God never leaves us, even when we're acting horrible, we just lose that protection He provides for us, because we are not following His guidance. I started listening to Him and as soon as I did, it started working. Now, it's like an addiction, I listen to Him about everything. I hope these things I learned help you find your way out of a bad situation.

There wasn't a day that went by in that old car that I didn't pray and I never miss a day now.

If you're facing bad times, please look at these things that worked for me. The one constant daily activity that you must do to survive bad times, and good times, is to pray. The power of prayer is amazing.

I CAN AND I WILL

CHAPTER FOURTEEN
A RELATIONSHIP WITH GOD

The first thing I had to do was to get a relationship with God. A friend of mine, Mike Huckabee, once said that faithfulness to the Lord is easy when things are horrible in your life, it's when times are good that it's the most difficult.

I'd never thought about this, but this is so true. I didn't pray much when I was a millionaire, but after I lost everything, I said multiple prayers daily. I was looking to Him for guidance and there's nothing wrong with that, but I had to continue to be just as faithful after I got back on my feet. This part has been easy for me. I pray multiple times daily, even when things are going great.

Religion was difficult for me because I wasn't brought up in a church environment and when I did go to church later in life, I felt horrible about myself when I left, so I didn't go much. I know this is not the right way to think, but it was easier to just not go. Although I wasn't going to church during this ordeal, nor did I ever think about it, I developed an extremely close relationship with God.

A couple of years later, Tina, Ricky and I walked into a church called A Simple Faith, and I never could have imagined the impact this place would have on me. A guy named Ronnie McBrayer was preaching in an old store front at a small strip mall. No signs. No pews. No crosses. Just a bunch of people listening to the greatest speaker I had ever heard. That sermon motivated me to do better. It also made me want to go to church for the first time in my life. He was like a regular person, not a normal preacher. The congregation didn't seem like a normal congregation. They didn't say much to us, but the love was overwhelming. I couldn't wait for the next Sunday! We had found our church and the people of A Simple Faith are my family now.

Sometimes, even though God has sent you a blessing, there will still be obstacles to overcome. One that I think of quite often is communion. Tina, Ricky and I walked with the congregation every week and took part in the sharing of the bread. I really didn't know what this was about, but it felt right to do it. Usually, if I was doing something wrong, I knew it was wrong, even if I came up with 20 reasons it was right to me. Here, this felt right.

Tina told a family member about our new church and I can still hear the excitement in her voice. When she got to the part about going through the communion line, the family member scolded her. She was told that it was against the"rules"for us to do that because we had never been baptised. Suddenly, I felt like we had broken a church code and God was going to strike us down immediately if we didn't repent. Tina was told that we must call our pastor and apologize and ask for forgiveness.

For a moment, I didn't want to go back to this church. I was scared to call Ronnie and tell him, so I sent an email. He replied quickly saying, "You All Keep Sharing In Communion!" I'm still not sure if we violated a cardinal rule, and whether Ronnie was just being nice, but we were baptised a few weeks later to be sure.

I'm also confused about praying, and I'm uncomfortable doing this in front of anyone else. I'm not sure there is a time that I'm more comfortable and at peace than when I'm praying alone. All I know is that I feel like I'm at home when I'm at A Simple Faith church and I feel closer to God when I'm there than any other time of the week.

To be successful, you must find a church that's right for you and your family. Without that fueling up of the soul, it's nearly impossible to be what God has blueprinted out for your life. I, like Ronnie, and many others at A Simple Faith, feel like we've complicated "the church" so much that we're nearly blocking the entry to everyone but the perfect, chosen few.

I could talk another five pages about the church. I'm sure many people may not agree and that's okay, as I am not scholarly regarding the Bible, but I feel that God is my buddy! It's pretty simple. God is talking to us every day. That voice you're hearing telling you that you're doing wrong is God. That voice telling you to help someone is God. As Mario Cuomo said, "Every time I've done something that doesn't feel right, it ended up not being right". This happens when we don't listen to our Heavenly Father.

I CAN AND I WILL

CHAPTER FIFTEEN
ACCEPT RESPONSIBILITY

Next, I had to accept the responsibility for my situation. I couldn't keep blaming others for my bad decisions.

Although there were bad people that did horrible things to us, I couldn't keep dwelling on those people and the things they had done. I had to push that blame away from them because there was absolutely nothing I could do about it. The only person that could do something about my bad decisions was me. If I didn't realize that I was responsible for my results and push forward, I was stuck. I had to make sure these things changed me because if they didn't, this was all wasted, and if anyone truly fails, it's because they didn't learn from their mistakes.

This sounds easy, but it's not. It's natural to blame others for anything that happens to us. If you'll think back to when you were a child and you took some candy from the kitchen that your mother told you not to eat before dinner, the first things out of your mouth were, "My brother did it too", or "My friend eats candy before dinner".

We really don't change much as we get older. We just modify our childish blame to fit the adult situation. If you're financially struggling, you'll never achieve success if you say things like, "My ex ran up my bills and left me with them", or "I was born poor and have never been given anything". I've used some of these excuses too. I noticed that as I slept in that old car in the first days, I was finding everyone to blame, and this was ok for a moment, because we were taken advantage of and I had to be cognizant of those things to ensure it didn't happen again.

But, once I accepted that I was the one that let it happen, things started to change. This may have been one of the most difficult obstacles I had to overcome, so make sure you pay attention. You must accept responsibility for your situation, because there's absolutely no path to success without doing this. I was the one that had achieved success and took it for granted. I was the one that was primarily to blame for where I was at, and where I had put my family.

It was only after this acceptance of responsibility that I moved to that next step that God was putting me in. It's essential to do this, whatever situation you're in.

CHAPTER SIXTEEN
STOP WAITING!

The next thing was to stop waiting on someone else to help. I had to get out of the "victim" mentality and remember we were "winners" having a bad moment.

I knew that this was not what God wanted for me, but I also had to remind myself constantly that although God is there for me, I had to take action myself, not wait on someone else. I had to realize that I was a grown man and sitting idle waiting on my family, friends, or the government to come bail me out of this horrible time of my life was not only stupid, but a self-righteous attitude to have regarding my state of mind.

Who the hell did I think I was? I had to get off my ass and fix this myself. I came to the realization that the only people on this earth who were going to work with me to get out of this predicament, were Tina and Ricky. And it wasn't right to even expect others to, because we were the ones in this mess.

Not many people are lucky enough to go through such dire times to see who is there, but I couldn't be more proud of my wife and son, as they stood by my side every day to see that we survived. It would have been easy for them to walk away without me, and most likely it was the best move for them, but it wasn't what was best for us three, our family.

No matter how loathsome the job or task we had in front of us to survive, we did it, and because of this time of our lives, there is a bond that will never be broken between us three.

I CAN AND I WILL

CHAPTER SEVENTEEN
CONFIDENCE

Next, we had to build our confidence back up. This may have been and still is the most difficult task in front of me.

Before all of this happened, I had a swagger to me. If I touched it, it was a success. I figured out how to make it a success. Now, I was in a situation that I could not make work. Although I did everything I could to keep my swagger, I lost it. Then I figured out a problem that too much confidence brings to a person. When you think you know everything, you stop learning because you think you already know the answer to every question or circumstance life throws at you.

I thought about this on night 2 and realized that I had to start learning again. Learn from everyone. Learn from the people doing good. Learn from the people doing bad. Learn. I started watching people and learning how they reacted to different situations. This helped me to slowly gain my confidence back.

I'm much more guarded now than I was before this ordeal. To build up our confidence, we threw multiple ideas, and "chances" out to the public and if you do this, some of them are going to be winners. In our case, we walked the streets gathering names to send postcards trying to get cleaning jobs. It worked! We called a realtor asking to mow a yard. It worked. We figured out little ways to solve the problems that those 10 days sprung on us. Every time we solved a problem, or an idea worked, it built our confidence.

We never talked about the things that didn't work. It was like we never tried them, but those failures served a purpose too. Even though we didn't talk about those failures, we learned from them, and moved on. You can't dwell on the fact that something didn't work the way you wanted it to. If we talked about the failures, it was giving them life, and we didn't want to give any more of our failures life to bring us down. We focused on the wins, and this was working. We started feeling like winners again.

I'll never be the guy I was before, nor do I want to be. My view on success and confidence has changed. I've changed.

Tina and I met Kelley and Debbie Mossburg in Auburn, Alabama. We talked for more than two hours discussing business, life and our beliefs. Kelley told me that ordeals like what Tina and I went through change people. They typically get angry and bitter or they become extremely kind and compassionate.

Our new goal in life is to help as many people as we can before we die. We are not going to let this part of our lives make us angry or bitter. We chose kindness and compassion. Now, it seems so simple.

CHAPTER EIGHTEEN
HOPE

We had to keep "Hope" alive, even when we were at our lowest point. This is different than confidence because hope is the dream of making something a reality.

After everything started swirling out of control, I never lost hope. I kept my mind working toward the right goal. One problem. I wasn't acting on that hope. It's not enough to simply hope, I had to take action with the gifts that God had given me.

I kept thinking that if I thought about it enough, it would get better and heal itself. To some extent, I had it right. If you stay focused and think about where you want to be, it helps, but the part I was missing was an extremely vital part. I had to act on those thoughts. We all have good and bad thoughts. Just as a bad thought must be clinched with a bad act to bring it to life, a good thought is the same way. You should act on those plans and hopes for a better life. Those good thoughts are God speaking to you. A successful person acts and memorializes those thoughts into a performance that God is proud of, and you'll always be rewarded.

In our case, we were in a horrible situation. At that moment, our hope was to get out of that car and get a roof back over our heads. We acted on our hopes and did everything that we needed to do to make this happen. I feel like we did it in a way that made God proud. We worked and we worked hard and followed His instructions precisely.

I CAN AND I WILL

CHAPTER NINETEEN
PREPARE FOR TESTS

Even when you're doing your best, there will be tests that the natural world will throw at you.

I was on the phone with a family member just a few months ago and she asked me how my day was going. I replied that I was exhausted and explained how hard we had worked preparing desserts for four weddings and a birthday party all in one day, while studying for law school exams. She told me, "Well, you're not used to working like that. You've never had to work hard."

Those words absolutely crushed me. The one thing that I took pride in my entire life was working hard. I believe that it's much easier for others, who have never taken that leap into the business world, to simply say "Oh well, they were lucky. Things just fell into place for them, and they made money", but this isn't typically true.

Most successful people have worked for it, even when we think they didn't. We want it to seem simple, like we're guarding that gate to success, not wanting to turn loose of our secrets. I had always made my family believe that my early success in life was easy, when in fact, it was not. I had never complained before about work to anyone. I had never told anyone how hard my family and I worked. The only people that really knew were Tina, Ricky and me, so maybe this is what everyone thought.

At that moment, I realized, it doesn't matter what anyone thinks. We can't be perfect, and I had to just keep working for God and moving forward. This conversation could have derailed my progress, and my path to success. I couldn't let this happen! I also learned from this talk that maybe I had done this to others. If I did, I had to make sure that I never did it again. I realized at that moment that I had to encourage others whenever I had the opportunity. Encouragement from family members and friends is essential to success. I learned that I must take every opportunity in the future to inspire and motivate everyone that I have a chance to help.

If you think about it, we all have these chances every day. Take advantage of them and respond with loving, inspirational words that make that person's day easier. Let them know how proud of them you are, and never insult anyone. Think about your words as they cannot be taken back. As insignificant as they may sound to you, they may be crushing to others. Make a point to be as kind as possible to everyone and it will not be a mistake.

Another hurdle that had to be jumped was the decision to stand up for what I believed or to cower and keep my job. As I will discuss in Chapter 20, at one time I took a job that was extremely instrumental to help get Tina, Ricky, and me back on our feet. I loved working there, and by the time the benefits, bonuses, and other things were considered, my salary was near $100,000 annually with a company car included. I loved the people I worked for and with. We were putting our life back together and all was great.

The family I worked for decided to sell the company. They sent the new leaders to meet the local supervisors, me included. While here, the company met with me and expressed its gratitude for the job I was doing, as my district had produced record-setting sales and profits. During the visit with me, God's name was used in vain on several occasions, but I let it go. The new group of employees used the same vulgarity.

For those who know me, I occasionally say a curse word, but I never use God's name in vain. After everything we had been through, to which I completely attribute our comeback to God, it was like a slap in the face every time he said this. I felt like I wasn't being faithful to God by not saying something, but I knew I needed this job. But, I politely told them that I didn't like the use of God's name in this manner. A representative met me at one of my stores the next day and he walked that store showing me everything that was wrong, while using God's name in vain the entire time. The store manager pulled him to the side and told him that he could curse, but please don't use that language because Rick didn't allow the employees to say it.

His response to her was "Well, let God pay his fu..... bills". The next morning I was called into the corporate office and fired. The manager of the store that told me what he said was fired a few weeks later.

This may have been one of the biggest tests that I had to pass to move on to my better life. I stood in the parking lot of that office, with no way to get home, no job, and feeling defeated. Then I realized that I didn't have a choice. I could not allow these words to keep being used or I could never move on to the next level in my life. So as defeated as I felt, I knew I did what had to be done.

At this time, Sweet Henrietta's was a part-time hobby that Tina was starting to make some extra money. After I was fired, we devoted our time to this project and before long we were making a six-figure income doing what we loved to do. I never missed that job one day, nor did we miss a bill because of it. It was like, other than the lessons learned, and the memories made, that job never existed.

My point is, if you stay faithful to God, as difficult as it may seem sometimes, you will be rewarded for your loyalty. God took that horrible experience and strained the bad from it, like it never happened. A faint memory of the dismissal remains in my mind, but most of the recollections I have now is of friendships made during the good times there. I don't regret confronting this man, in fact, I'm proud of the dedication to God that I displayed and there's no doubt I was rewarded for it.

A few years later, we sold that business for a decent amount of money and continue to devote our lives to doing better and living for God.

CHAPTER TWENTY
GIVE

Another aspect of getting back on our feet and living the life that God had planned was to give. As difficult as this may seem, when you're homeless, it wasn't.

As we slept in that car, it made us want to help others. It's kind of like we all do. As soon as we cannot do something, we want to do it. I'm proud of my family, because every day we had a conversation about helping people when we got back on our feet.

Then it occurred to us, why are we talking about giving after we got back on our feet? That's like saying, God, if you'll make things better, then I'll do better. We could give now, we just had to be a little more creative. If I could make someone feel better, feel good, or feel inspired, they'd never forget that. They may forget everything I'd ever said to them, but they'll never forget how I could make them feel. That's a powerful gift we all hold, I just had to genuinely care about others to use it.

Listening, giving and so many other attributes we are born with fade away with out use. A lot of love I had for humankind when I was a child had slowly melted away as I grew into an adult. I noticed the more I loved others, the easier it got again. So now, if I didn't have money to give, I could still listen to others concerns, worries and stories.

I learned that the more I listened to them, we all shared the same problems, just with different variables injected. It was never completely about us, but the ability to help was our primary motivator during those 10 days of homelessness. It was easy to donate money when I had lots of money. Many times, we focus on the money when referring to giving.

Giving is exactly what it says. The giving of yourself to a Godly cause. Sometimes the giving that is most appreciated by God is your time. Sometimes, it is money. It's difficult to explain but easy when it's happening and the need is there in front of you. You'll know perfectly well what He is telling you to do. I believe that our world has limited giving to only those that "deserve it", when none of us deserve the good that God has done already. We don't give in fear that the person we're giving to doesn't deserve it, need it, or it is a scam.

Always be cognizant of a potential fraud, but don't worry too much about it. If you're giving with your heart, you didn't do wrong. It's the person you are giving to who must deal with those consequences, not you.

I thought a lot about what to do to make the world better, when I normally didn't think much about that before. I thought about others with no transportation, no home, no food, and no family living nearby. I didn't have money to give, but that shouldn't keep me from giving back.

I noticed something I never noticed before. The more good I did, and thought, the more good things were returned to me. I had to be really careful here because good and giving has to come from the heart, and not stemmed from an expectation for something in return.

During those 10 days in that old car, we did things like take shopping carts inside from the parking lot, stop and talk to elderly people, pick up litter from store floors, give a part of our food to a homeless person on the side of the road, and most importantly, we were genuinely concerned about the welfare of everyone struggling.

Tina and I talk a lot about these things, and we never expected to get anything in return for doing those deeds, but thinking back, we did. We were blessed more often when we were giving back to the world that our God has blessed us with. I noticed that the more I gave, the more I received. This was dangerous, because now, occasionally I'll give and in the back of my mind, I think "Oh, I'm going to receive something in return for this." You should be thoughtful of your state of mind.

Giving is always good, but typically, if you can hardly notice that you've given something, there's not much effort in it. I don't believe anyone will ever go broke from giving. I think God has made sure of that.

A couple of years ago, a family member called and told me that someone in my family needed some money. They had no idea of what Tina, Ricky and I had been through, and I didn't tell. They asked if I could send $1,000 to this person. I immediately, without thinking, said I could. The only problem was, Tina and I only had about $1,500 to our name. I told Tina about this, and she agreed. We had to send the money and we did.

By this time, I had taken on a job at a locally owned chain of convenience stores and there was a potential bonus that was paid every month. Typically, there was not a bonus paid, but even if you got one, most of the time, it was minimal because of the stipulations to get it. This month, I was paid a $6,000 bonus. It was the largest bonus ever given by this company. I believe that you must give until it hurts to get to that special place God has chosen for you in this world.

I CAN AND I WILL

CHAPTER TWENTY-ONE
APPRECIATE

Always appreciate others, not only for what they've done for you, but what they've done to live a Godly life. Here, it was easy to do. Sadly, when you're broke, not many people come around you or call.

I have immense appreciation for my friend, Don Garner. During the 10 days we lived in a car, Don was the only person who called just to check on me. He was the only one to call just to say "I love you". Everyone else had an agenda except him and I'll never forget it. Be that person who calls just to say you love them. Be that person who sincerely cares about the welfare of another with no hidden agenda for yourself. Be a Don Garner.

Now, it's not fair to blame anyone for not calling because nobody had any idea how dire our situation was, not even Don, but not many people figure out the needs of others without the person in need asking. We never told anyone. We live in a world where "losing everything" means only having $1 million in the bank and selling your Porsche to drive a Toyota. In our case, we literally lost nearly everything we had.

I noticed during this time, and even today, that my appreciation for things people do is stronger. I appreciate that guy who cooks my lunch at Burger King. I appreciate the cashier, janitor, police officer, teacher, firefighter and other people who serve us daily. Even if they are not nice, I appreciate them and understand that maybe they're having a hard day. I appreciate my father, mother, brother, other family members and friends. I think back about little things my parents, and grandparents did for me, that I didn't think much about then.

And, mostly, I appreciate God. If you don't appreciate the gifts

God has given you, you'll never reach your full potential. Now that you've started appreciating others, you must appreciate everything. Tina and I started appreciating crazy, little things like a discount on gasoline. We would actually thank God when things like this happened. It seemed like after we started doing this, other things started falling in to place. God knew what was in my heart, but after I started saying the words – "Thank You Lord", after little wins, I felt better and somehow, I knew that He wanted to hear that.

So now, I thank God for everything. If a lane opens up in traffic, I thank God. If the soda I'm buying at Tom Thumb is free, I'm thanking God. I can't explain how much I appreciate God working with us, obviously our entire lives, but I truly believe He was sleeping with us in that old car every night. He was there when Tina was injured with that needle and when I was at the beach alone, and wanted to die. I'm absolutely convinced that He saved us from dying and kept my family together.

I had to change my mindset. I had no idea that I was living a negative life until I thought about these issues. I had to change my mentality on paying bills, from a hardship to a blessing. I had to change my way of thinking regarding grocery shopping. The ability to purchase groceries is a true blessing, not a hindrance.

Not very long ago, Tina and I didn't have money for groceries, so Praise God! Appreciate everything, and you'll have everything you need.

CHAPTER TWENTY-TWO
POSITIVITY

Surround yourself with people you want to be like and stay away from those that hinder your advancement of God's work.

Most people don't realize this about me, but I'm easily influenced. If someone I like tells me something, I believe it and before long, I'm thinking the same way. I thought this was a horrible personality trait, but I've used it to benefit my life. I still believe everyone, I just limit myself to good, thoughtful, energetic, positive people. If I must talk to a negative person, I listen for a moment and move on before my mind is clouded with their negativity.

We all have those people in our lives who are always negative and some that are down right hateful at the world. You must limit your contact to people who make your path to success more difficult. Don't let these people distract you from doing good.

I told myself for many years that I could help people with bad attitudes and they just needed to vent their frustrations with life. That can happen for a while, but you'll notice if someone is a habitual complainer, they cannot be helped until they choose to change. You can't help a person who does not see an issue with their actions, so if you continue to try, before long, they change you and then God's plans are altered until you get back on the right path.

In my case, I had to stop communicating with people who hate or gossip about others. I found myself feeling the same way they did, and doing the same things with absolutely no reason, other than their words. I also had to not be that person who manipulates others, or gossips, hates, and is negative when speaking with people. To be that person God wants me to be, I had to surround myself with positive influences who are living the life that I want to live. I had to cut ties with many people that I love and I would still do anything in the world for. I found that I could not cloud my mind with those negative thoughts.

I still talk with people who do this, but I limit the length of my conversation. Before long, those people don't call anymore. They get their fuel/energy from people agreeing with them. God will reward you for staying faithful to His word. I figured out during these 10 Days that I could feed off the energy of others. I knew that I had to stay positive, but I also remembered my successful past and how I achieved it. I hung out with successful people, even when I was young and broke. I soaked in everything they said. I watched and mimicked their behavior. Back then, I was completely focused on money, and that was what my target was. Although I needed money, and needed it badly, I needed to change and this is much more difficult than making money.

Most people want to get better and change their way of living, but not many people do it. People tend to change during their time of need, and then after God steps in and saves them, they go right back to the same person they were before. I could not let this happen. I had to be one of the few that changed my life by changing myself and this is not easy. I needed to find happiness, hope, and goodness that I had never had before.

Now, my situation had changed. I was older. Even though I was broke back then, you're supposed to be broke when you're in your 20s, not when you're 38 years old. I had to look to people for guidance, not only in a financial manner, but also in the way they lived their life. I needed to find goal oriented, happy, eccentric, successful friends to surround myself with. This sounds easy, but not so simple when you're sleeping in a car.

I found my guidance in some people I had known for years like Don Garner. Don and I had been friends for a long time. He worked at a horse stable when I met him and I'd go out to visit him while he was feeding horses and cleaning the barns. One day Don asked me what I thought about him quitting his job and selling cars for a living. Now, you should understand that although Don was working at a horse stable, he made good money. I told him I thought he should do it while everyone else was against it. The reason I told Don to take the leap was because I knew that if he didn't try, he'd regret it. I also knew that he was good with people and I truly had faith he would be successful. Now, Don sells millions of dollars in cars and brings in a hefty salary as one of the elite car salesmen in the area.

Another person I looked to for guidance was Bert Summerville. Bert hired Tina and me to clean houses. Now that sounds insignificant, but it wasn't. Bert was a tremendously successful real estate agent and after I'd clean a house she owned, I would talk to her regarding business and run creative ideas by her. Most people didn't pay much attention to the cleaning crew. She would always listen, as I would soak in everything she said regarding business and creative, alternative ideas in entrepreneurship.

I also learned not to act like some of the people I met. I remember cleaning a condominium for a guy who treated Tina and me like we were second-class citizens. I was extremely grateful for the work, but one day, he insulted us by yelling negative comments over the phone. The reason was because the electricity was out in his condo and guests were coming soon. There was an electrical problem and I worked for 30 minutes trying to repair the issue. I knew that God had put people like this in my life to make sure I understood the hurt caused by them. I learned that under no circumstance could I ever talk down to someone working, especially when there was no reason. I learned from this angry man, that I couldn't be angry and advance to that next level.

I was like a 3-year-old child learning things for the first time. I soaked in all this behavior, good and bad. I knew that I had to take the good and apply it to my new life and I also had to take those bad things, and make sure I didn't let them happen. Each person I met, I learned from and used their personalities to help me move out of the spot I was in.

Just because I've distanced myself from a person, does not indicate that I do not love them. I don't have a choice. If I kept filling my head with these thoughts, I could not fulfill the life God wants for me. I truly believe that all people are inherently good, it's just that something happens to people along the track of life and it burdens them to a point of anger and manipulation. When this happens, the only path to righteousness is through Jesus Christ. There's no other way!

CHAPTER TWENTY-THREE
FORGIVE

Forgive. This may have been the most difficult aspect of success for me.

During our hard times, although I have accepted responsibility for it, there were people who took advantage of my situation. People who literally took our last pennies to benefit themselves. People who stopped calling when I couldn't benefit them any longer.

I felt like people were angry at me because I couldn't financially help them anymore. This may have not been the case... maybe they were embarrassed for me and didn't know what to say if they called.

I had to forgive the people who had done these things to my family. You must let go. The success that you will achieve soon is much more satisfying without carrying around the anger or resentment for others. In fact, it is absolutely essential that you let go and forgive.

Without this forgiveness, you cannot move forward. How can I expect someone to forgive me, if I can't even forgive others? It makes no sense to haul this burden around with you. Let go of it and the quicker you do, the quicker you'll achieve that life God has ready for you.

Ask for forgiveness. At the same time I was forgiving others, I had to be mindful of the people I had hurt. I had people depending on me for many things, and I let them down. Although I had to accept that I couldn't do those things any longer, I needed them to understand that I was sorry for the things that I did to hurt them. It's important to ask for forgiveness, but it is not essential that they forgive you for you to move on.

God knows your heart's intention and He is the only one we

ultimately must please. Once you ask, and your heart is right with God, you're good. Move on.

CHAPTER TWENTY-FOUR
BELIEVE AND SUCCEED

Believe. This keeps so many people from achieving their dreams.

I was raised in a small town and poverty was normal. The possibilities were so limited that my yearning for a better life was not guaranteed and there was no place to go but up. But, as far back as I can remember, I believed in a bright future. It is easy when you're young and broke, but it became more difficult when I achieved success and lost it.

Then, believing for a brighter tomorrow, even though it still took the same mindset, was almost impossible for me to do. On Day 4, I knew that I had to truly believe that I could succeed again. When Tina and I took long walks and we looked at multi-million dollar homes, we forced ourselves to believe that we could get one again.

When we read about Bill Gates donating millions, we pictured ourselves being able to do the same thing. When we saw people returning home from missionary trips to other countries, we began to talk about us doing the same thing. Make your mind believe that you are capable of doing what you're wanting to achieve. The more you talk about, read, dream, and live the things you want, you'll eventually train your mind to believe it can be achieved.

I had to truly believe that my life was going to be beneficial to humankind and our earth. I started believing that I was supplied gifts from God that could help others succeed and excel. Now, act on your new mindset and set of beliefs.

Don't be afraid to fail. I was raised in a family and community that only viewed blue-collar work as real work. If you weren't driving a tractor, digging a ditch, building a house, and sweating you were not working. This limited my mindset early on to only look for careers in blue-collar industries. I say this as a blue-collar worker and I am proud to be one. But I had to step outside that frame of thinking to move forward.

You must have the courage to, as Steve Harvey would say, "jump". That was easy when I was young, but later, I began to change into what the world said was acceptable. When I was young, and especially after my failure, I had to build that confidence up again and realize that failure was not the end of the world. When I say, don't be afraid to fail, I mean don't let it consume you to the point that you don't even try. You can be scared, but use that fright to motivate your success. It frightened me more to work at a regular job for 30 years and then retire from it than to attempt other things and fail.

I don't regret any choice I made. I consider myself lucky to have a story to tell. If I had never jumped into life with a distinct possibility of failure, I would not have this story to tell. I consider living a life without a story more of a failure than losing everything after you jumped.

Now, that being said, there's absolutely nothing wrong with working a normal job and retiring after 30 years, and that option looked extremely appealing as I slept in that old car for 10 days. A little scared is not a bad thing. Many people were quick to judge when I lost everything, and were eager to say things like – "he should have just gotten a real job", or "get a job like everyone else".

I had to let this go and regain my confidence, stop worrying about what others thought and immediately stop being consumed with failure. God does not want us to be scared because if we have true confidence in Him, we will succeed.

CHAPTER TWENTY-FIVE
LISTEN AND LAUGH

Listen to the people God has put in front of you. I would talk to very few people during our 10 days of homelessness. The few people I did talk to, if they had listened to my words, and what I told them, they most likely would have known that things were tough. I'm not sure if I had always been like this, or if it was a new benefit I acquired after I lost everything.

I listened to people. I listened to someone talking to me about being sick, or being happy. I noticed that if I asked questions about what they were talking about, they were immediately happy and eager to talk more about their life and most of the time, they were surprised that I was really listening.

I also noticed that most people don't listen to what you're saying. They immediately change the story and insert themselves into their own story to tell you. This is natural to happen occasionally, but if you continue to do it, it takes away from your ability to learn from others and grow into the child of God you need to be to achieve success.

I had to listen to others to get out of the mess I was in, not waste time talking about the mess I had created. I had to learn. I had to figure this out and it was not going to be on my own.

I also recalled conversations I had during my entire life and applied those to my ability to grow and learn from my mistakes. I knew that God had given me the wisdom through these people He had placed in my life over the years, I just had to use it. As soon as we think we have all the answers ourselves, without the help or input of others, we've failed before we start.

Laugh. The months leading up to our 10 days, we didn't laugh much. We figured this out on Day 3. We laughed about a conversation we were having and it felt therapeutic. Immediately after this silly conversation, I was filled with happiness, even after I had lost everything. I figured out instantly that I had to let go of the guilt and laugh. The more I could enhance my spirit with laughter, the quicker I could get my family out of this mess. In fact, it would not happen if I couldn't laugh.

No matter what had happened, I should not be doomed to a life of misery, and that is not what God wants. After this night, I tried to make sure that I made Tina laugh every day. A couple of days later, we laughed very hard about those lava rocks in the oven. That crazy idea I had was ridiculous, but the laughter we gained from it was priceless, and may have saved us because we had much more trouble to face before we got out of that old car.

I had felt like I didn't deserve to laugh. I had let people down who were depending on me, so how could I even think about laughing. How could a guy laugh who was a millionaire the year before and now sleeping in a car? If I didn't figure out a way to start laughing again, and keep laughing, there was no path to my new Godly life.

Don't go a day without laughter, and when you're facing turbulent times in life, figure out a way to laugh about something. Don't worry about what people think about your laughter. They'll probably think you're crazy. Laugh anyway.

CHAPTER TWENTY-SIX
DON'T BE THE JUDGE

Stop judging other people.

I come from a small town in southeast Missouri, so if anyone knows about small town life, you know that it's part of your life to judge everyone. I'll guarantee that the town drunk is judging the preacher and the preacher is judging the town drunk while, in some towns, they're the same guy.

Now, this was a way of life for me. I automatically judged people by the clothes they wore to the grammar they used. Even as I slept in a car, I had not stopped this horrible habit, and I'm not sure if I will ever be able to completely refrain from automatically doing it, but I'm much better about it now. Sleeping in a car made me realize that bad things happen to good people. To succeed and dig my way out of this mess, I had to stop.

But don't confuse expressing an opinion with being judgmental. There is absolutely nothing wrong with expressing an opinion. The difference is that we shouldn't look down on anyone for a superficial, outward, subjective trait they have. Those 10 days in a car made me realize that I had no idea what a person may be going through, so who was I to judge them for their shirt being dirty that day, or being in a bad mood.

I know I suggest that staying positive is a key to success, but I could not condemn someone for falling into a depression caused by life circumstances that I am not aware of. In my mind, God created all people good, so I'm going to treat them with respect, no matter what their outward appearance or attitude reflects.

I figured out how to mask my situation, but that situation also made me realize that people go through difficult times and sometimes they need help. I had to stop being judgmental to get to that level of success that God wanted for me. There's no path to grace through telling others how bad they are and there never will be.

Focus on yourself, your family, and helping others to get out of those roadblocks they've come across, not making them feel worse about what they've done.

CHAPTER TWENTY-SEVEN
PRAY

Lastly, Pray.

I've always been a little confused about religion. The only thing I'm sure of is that I believe in God, and I'm positive that God is good. He is the goodness that is in everyday life and that little voice telling you to do good. He is all around us, but we must want to see and hear him. Now, I'll end my story with a prayer.

Dear Lord,

I ask you to forgive me for the bad things I've done. I ask for you to help guide my thoughts, in this crazy world, to do good for others and live this life You've blessed me with to make You proud.

Help me to not judge others, as it is not my place to do so, and to love in your likeness the best I can. Please help me to listen to your children, my brothers and sisters and recognize their need. If there is something I can do to help them, please give me the wisdom to do it, just as You would.

Please give me the ability to learn from my mistakes and not to relive them and to forgive those who have hurt me. Please help me to make the people I have hurt to understand that I'm sorry and I have learned from those mistakes.

I want to thank You for my family, friends, and this life You've given me. It is because of You that I am here and I'm going to do the best I can to simply do good for the rest of my life.

Thank you. Amen

I truly believe that every one of these steps I've discussed is essential to digging our way out of holes we fall into while living our lives, or to make the correct decision when confronted with life choices. Life is not easy, and these steps, as simple as they sound, are extremely difficult to make.

Everyone goes through obstacles and life circumstances when we can either make right or wrong decisions. Everyone does not let it swirl out of control as badly as I did to the point that they're sleeping in a car, but everybody goes through troubling times, especially those who venture out into the world and try alternative, non-traditional ways to make a living.

In my case, I was more scared of living a "normal" life than I was of failure. Then, when I lost everything, I longed for that "normal" life I had avoided my entire life.

I came to realize that every person God created has a unique purpose while we live, but all also share one common characteristic that God demands of us. God wants us to prosper. God wants us to do good! While we're here, we must do good.

During my troubling period, I had to go through this horrible time of my life to figure out the things God intended for me to do. Each day of my homelessness, I was faced with problems that forced me to change to survive. I want to share those things that my family and I figured out for one reason, and that is to help others. Those 10 days at the beach ended up being the best 10 days of my life.

I am blessed with a new life because of those 10 days that I could have never achieved without them. I hope you find my story inspirational and it motivates you to work toward the life God has planned for you and that you are a blessing to everyone you meet.

What an honor to serve such a powerful and good God!

ABOUT THE AUTHOR

Rick Stanfield is a former Missouri State Trooper and entrepreneur who cofounded Sweet Henrietta's Treats in Santa Rosa Beach, Florida. Rick is a writer and authored the cookbook, "It's All Good". He is a law school graduate, who plans on spending the rest of his life helping people going through difficult times by sharing his story and doing whatever God calls him to do.